Francis Frith's
AROUND SUFFOLK

PHOTOGRAPHIC MEMORIES

Francis Frith's
AROUND SUFFOLK

◆

Clive Tully

FRITH
BOOK Co

First published in the United Kingdom in 1999 by
Frith Book Company Ltd

Hardback Edition 1999
ISBN 1-85937-074-8

Reprinted in Hardback 2001
ISBN 1-85937-074-8

Reprinted in Paperback 2002
ISBN 1-85937-221-x

British Library Cataloguing in Publication Data

Francis Frith's Around Suffolk
Clive Tully

Frith Book Company Ltd
Frith's Barn, Teffont,
Salisbury, Wiltshire SP3 5QP
Tel: +44 (0) 1722 716 376
Email: info@francisfrith.co.uk
www.francisfrith.co.uk

Printed and bound in Great Britain

CONTENTS

FRANCIS FRITH: *Victorian Pioneer*

FRANCIS FRITH, Victorian founder of the world-famous photographic archive, was a complex and multitudinous man. A devout Quaker and a highly successful Victorian businessman, he was both philosophic by nature and pioneering in outlook.

By 1855 Francis Frith had already established a wholesale grocery business in Liverpool, and sold it for the astonishing sum of £200,000, which is the equivalent today of over £15,000,000. Now a multi-millionaire, he was able to indulge his passion for travel. As a child he had pored over travel books written by early explorers, and his fancy and imagination had been stirred by family holidays to the sublime mountain regions of Wales and Scotland. 'What a land of spirit-stirring and enriching scenes and places!' he had written. He was to return to these scenes of grandeur in later years to 'recapture the thousands of vivid and tender memories', but with a different purpose. Now in his thirties, and captivated by the new science of photography, Frith set out on a series of pioneering journeys to the Nile regions that occupied him from 1856 until 1860.

INTRIGUE AND ADVENTURE

He took with him on his travels a specially-designed wicker carriage that acted as both dark-room and sleeping chamber. These far-flung journeys were packed with intrigue and adventure. In his life story, written when he was sixty-three, Frith tells of being held captive by bandits, and of fighting 'an awful midnight battle to the very point of surrender with a deadly pack of hungry, wild dogs'. Sporting flowing Arab costume, Frith arrived at Akaba by camel seventy years before Lawrence, where he encountered 'desert princes and rival sheikhs, blazing with jewel-hilted swords'.

During these extraordinary adventures he was assiduously exploring the desert regions bordering the Nile and patiently recording the antiquities and peoples with his camera. He was the first photographer to venture beyond the sixth cataract. Africa was still the mysterious 'Dark Continent', and Stanley and Livingstone's historic meeting was a decade into the future. The conditions for picture taking confound belief. He laboured for hours in his wicker dark-room in the sweltering heat of the desert, while the volatile chemicals fizzed dangerously in their trays. Often he was forced to work in remote tombs and caves where conditions were cooler. Back in London he exhibited his photographs and was 'rapturously cheered' by members of the Royal Society. His reputation as a photographer was made overnight. An eminent modern historian has likened their impact on the population of the time to that on our own generation of the first photographs taken on the surface of the moon.

VENTURE OF A LIFE-TIME

Characteristically, Frith quickly spotted the opportunity to create a new business as a specialist publisher of photographs. He lived in an era of immense and sometimes violent change. For the poor in the early part of Victoria's reign work was a drudge and the hours long, and people had precious little free time to enjoy themselves.

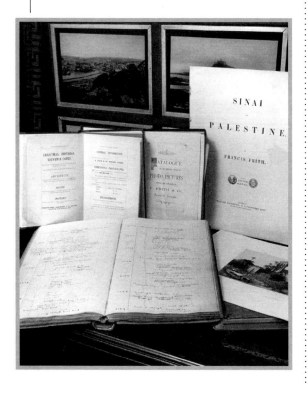

Most had no transport other than a cart or gig at their disposal, and had not travelled far beyond the boundaries of their own town or village. However, by the 1870s, the railways had threaded their way across the country, and Bank Holidays and half-day Saturdays had been made obligatory by Act of Parliament. All of a sudden the ordinary working man and his family were able to enjoy days out and see a little more of the world.

With characteristic business acumen, Francis Frith foresaw that these new tourists would enjoy having souvenirs to commemorate their days out. In 1860 he married Mary Ann Rosling and set out with the intention of photographing every city, town and village in Britain. For the next thirty years he travelled the country by train and by pony and trap, producing fine photographs of seaside resorts and beauty spots that were keenly bought by millions of Victorians. These prints were painstakingly pasted into family albums and pored over during the dark nights of winter, rekindling precious memories of summer excursions.

THE RISE OF FRITH & CO

Frith's studio was soon supplying retail shops all over the country. To meet the demand he gathered about him a small team of photographers, and published the work of independent artist-photographers of the calibre of Roger Fenton and Francis Bedford. In order to gain some understanding of the scale of Frith's business one only has to look at the catalogue issued by Frith & Co in 1886: it runs to some 670

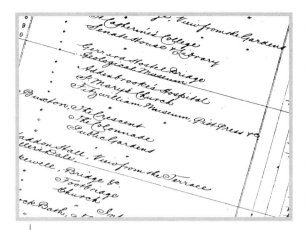

pages, listing not only many thousands of views of the British Isles but also many photographs of most European countries, and China, Japan, the USA and Canada – note the sample page shown above from the hand-written *Frith & Co* ledgers detailing pictures taken. By 1890 Frith had created the greatest specialist photographic publishing company in the world, with over 2,000 outlets – more than the combined number that Boots and WH Smith have today! The picture on the right shows the *Frith & Co* display board at Ingleton in the Yorkshire Dales. Beautifully constructed with mahogany frame and gilt inserts, it could display up to a dozen local scenes.

POSTCARD BONANZA

◆◆

The ever-popular holiday postcard we know today took many years to develop. In 1870 the Post Office issued the first plain cards, with a pre-printed stamp on one face. In 1894 they allowed other publishers' cards to be sent through the mail with an attached adhesive halfpenny stamp. Demand grew rapidly, and in 1895 a new size of postcard was permitted called the

court card, but there was little room for illustration. In 1899, a year after Frith's death, a new card measuring 5.5 x 3.5 inches became the standard format, but it was not until 1902 that the divided back came into being, with address and message on one face and a full-size illustration on the other. *Frith & Co* were in the vanguard of postcard development, and Frith's sons Eustace and Cyril continued their father's monumental task, expanding the number of views offered to the public and recording more and more places in Britain, as the coasts and countryside were opened up to mass travel.

Francis Frith died in 1898 at his villa in Cannes, his great project still growing. The archive he created continued in business for another seventy years. By 1970 it contained over a third of a million pictures of 7,000 cities, towns and villages. The massive photographic record Frith has left to us stands as a living monument to a special and very remarkable man.

Frith's Archive: *A Unique Legacy*

FRANCIS FRITH'S legacy to us today is of immense significance and value, for the magnificent archive of evocative photographs he created provides a unique record of change in 7,000 cities, towns and villages throughout Britain over a century and more. Frith and his fellow studio photographers revisited locations many times down the years to update their views, compiling for us an enthralling and colourful pageant of British life and character.

We tend to think of Frith's sepia views of Britain as nostalgic, for most of us use them to conjure up memories of places in our own lives with which we have family associations. It often makes us forget that to Francis Frith they were records of daily life as it was actually being lived in the cities, towns and villages of his day. The Victorian age was one of great and often bewildering change for ordinary people, and though the pictures evoke an impression of slower times, life was as busy and hectic as it is today.

We are fortunate that Frith was a photographer of the people, dedicated to recording the minutiae of everyday life. For it is this sheer wealth of visual data, the painstaking chronicle of changes in dress, transport, street layouts, buildings, housing, engineering and landscape that captivates us so much today. His remarkable images offer us a powerful link with the past and with the lives of our ancestors.

TODAY'S TECHNOLOGY

Computers have now made it possible for Frith's many thousands of images to be accessed almost instantly. In the Frith archive today, each photograph is carefully 'digitised' then stored on a CD Rom. Frith archivists can locate a single photograph amongst thousands within seconds. Views can be catalogued and sorted under a variety of categories of place and content to the immediate benefit of researchers. Inexpensive reference prints can be created for them at the touch of a mouse button, and a wide range of books and other printed materials assembled and published for a wider, more general readership - in the next twelve months over a hundred Frith local history titles will be published! The

See Frith at www.francisfrith.co.uk

day-to-day workings of the archive are very different from how they were in Francis Frith's time: imagine the herculean task of sorting through eleven tons of glass negatives as Frith had to do to locate a particular sequence of pictures! Yet the archive still prides itself on maintaining the same high standards of excellence laid down by Francis Frith, including the painstaking cataloguing and indexing of every view.

It is curious to reflect on how the internet now allows researchers in America and elsewhere greater instant access to the archive than Frith himself ever enjoyed. Many thousands of individual views can be called up on screen within seconds on one of the Frith internet sites, enabling people living continents away to revisit the streets of their ancestral home town, or view places in Britain where they have enjoyed holidays. Many overseas researchers welcome the chance to view special theme selections, such as transport, sports, costume and ancient monuments.

We are certain that Francis Frith would have heartily approved of these modern developments, for he himself was always working at the very limits of Victorian photographic technology.

THE VALUE OF THE ARCHIVE TODAY

Because of the benefits brought by the computer, Frith's images are increasingly studied by social historians, by researchers into genealogy and ancestory, by architects, town planners, and by teachers and schoolchildren involved in local history projects. In addition, the archive offers every one of us a unique opportunity to examine the places where we and our families have lived and worked down the years. Immensely successful in Frith's own era, the archive is now, a century and more on, entering a new phase of popularity.

THE PAST IN TUNE WITH THE FUTURE

Historians consider the Francis Frith Collection to be of prime national importance. It is the only archive of its kind remaining in private ownership and has been valued at a million pounds. However, this figure is now rapidly increasing as digital technology enables more and more people around the world to enjoy its benefits.

Francis Frith's archive is now housed in an historic timber barn in the beautiful village of Teffont in Wiltshire. Its founder would not recognize the archive office as it is today. In place of the many thousands of dusty boxes containing glass plate negatives and an all-pervading odour of photographic chemicals, there are now ranks of computer screens. He would be amazed to watch his images travelling round the world at unimaginable speeds through network and internet lines.

The archive's future is both bright and exciting. Francis Frith, with his unshakeable belief in making photographs available to the greatest number of people, would undoubtedly approve of what is being done today with his lifetime's work. His photographs, depicting our shared past, are now bringing pleasure and enlightenment to millions around the world a century and more after his death.

SUFFOLK – *An Introduction*

To MANY, SUFFOLK might bring to mind the characterful colour-washed timber-framed houses of places like Lavenham or Kersey, or the soaring splendour of its churches. To others it might be that unique quality of light found on the coast at places like Southwold, and at Aldeburgh, which so inspired the composer Benjamin Britten. Along the coast, Walberswick proved a magnet to a whole host of distinguished artists, such as Charles Rennie Mackintosh and Stanley Spencer.

With Norfolk to the north, Essex to the south and Cambridgeshire to the west, Suffolk occupies the middle part of that distinctive bulge in the east coast of Britain. The boundaries are fairly straightforward topographically speaking. To the north, the boundary is the rivers Waveney and Little Ouse, to the south, the River Stour, while in the west, it is largely where the more rolling Suffolk countryside meets the flat fens of Cambridgeshire.

Suffolk has some fifty miles of coastline, much of it with beautiful heaths as its hinterland. Over the centuries, the shape of the coastline has changed considerably. Towns like Aldeburgh, Dunwich and Covehithe have all suffered from erosion. It is hard to imagine that the tiny hamlet that remains of Dunwich is but a tiny part of what was once one of the country's major ports. Elsewhere, the coastline has built up: Orford, for example, was once open to the sea, and is now separated from it by a long spit of shingle which formed due to a process called longshore drift. Generally, the fact that Suffolk's coastline is all low-lying has put it at risk from tidal surges - the worst being the 1953 floods which affected much of the East Coast.

Just over 900 years ago, at the time of the Domesday Survey of 1086, Suffolk was one of the most densely populated areas in the country. There were just a few large towns, but over 400 villages. William rewarded various nobles who had helped him with the conquest by awarding them numerous manors. Three powerful families had the lion's share of Suffolk between them, but by the middle of the 12th century, it was the ambitious Bigod family who controlled the county. Henry II countered the threat by building the castle at Orford, and attacking Framlingham castle.

Between the time of the conquest and Henry VIII, it was the religious orders who held sway. They became the landowners, imposing not just rents on their tenants, but taxes as well. It was the provocation of such taxes that led to the abbey of St Edmundsbury being burned down in 1327. In the 13th century, many English barons believed in certain principles of government, drawing up a charter which they wanted King John to ratify. On the 20th November 1214, they met at Bury St Edmunds abbey church in secret, and swore an oath to compel the king to sign, by force if

tled here when sheep farming was at its height, and created a wool industry which became world-famous. As a result, many buildings in East Anglia have a pronounced Dutch influence. At the peak of the industry, Suffolk was producing more wool than any other county in England, with various local variations of heavy broadcloth (the best known came from Kersey) exported all over Europe. By the reign of Elizabeth I, however, heavy broadcloths had gone out of fashion,

necessary. As twenty-five barons secretly plotting against the king might not be favourably regarded in some quarters, it was logical that they should choose to meet here, at an important place of pilgrimage, where they hoped that their assembly would go unnoticed. The king signed the following year, at Runnymede, and the Magna Carta has formed the basis of government of this country ever since.

Over the centuries, a number of different industries have kept Suffolk prosperous. In medieval times, the backbone of industry in the area was the wool and cloth-weaving trade. Many Dutch and Flemish weavers set-

replaced by lighter and more colourful fabrics. While Sudbury managed to adapt and turn out fine silks, many Suffolk towns lost the opportunity to adapt to the changing circumstances. When the first power looms were invented - devices relying on fast running water to provide the power - the textile industry moved north to the Pennines, and when coal became the fuel for industry in the 19th century, the textile factories were already well placed to utilise it.

Suffolk had a thriving fishing industry as well; the herring trade in particular made the fortunes of several coastal towns. But the changing shape of the coastline played its part, too. As medieval ports silted up, so the fishermen turned to other forms of fishing. Lowestoft retained its importance as a fishing port, although latter years have seen a decline due to European fishing quotas.

Agriculture has always been a part of the Suffolk landscape, and there were times in history when it was doubtless very profitable, evidenced by some of the huge brick barns which can still be found around the county, even if most have been converted into characterful dwellings in the recent years. Suffolk's rich pastures proved good for grazing cattle and sheep, and the abundance of oak forests meant that there was plenty of oak bark, an essential component of tanning. So it was that many Suffolk towns profited from the leather industry, which shipped goods as far away as India.

The coming of the railway in the 19th century undoubtedly changed the face of the region. Although the sailing barges which carried goods up and down the east coast carried on into the early 20th century, the trains started to eat into their business. But the biggest changes came simply with the movement of people. Towns like Lowestoft and Felixstowe became tourist resorts, and many developments followed rapidly.

Churches in Suffolk give a fascinating insight into the past, and the people who built them. Many villages and towns celebrated their prosperity from wool in this way (building and decorating their churches undoubtedly eased their consciences), but others were paid for by the profits from fishing, plundering and military gains. The majority of Suffolk churches date from the mid-14th to the 15th century, the Perpendicular period, with contrasting stone and patterned flint flushwork. The churches were decorated lavishly inside, too, with wall paintings illustrating religious themes. But the most brightly decorated objects, the rood screens built across the naves of many churches, fell victim to Henry VIII's ban on such objects of veneration. The greatest Puritanism came during the Cromwellian period, when walls were whitewashed, and all kinds of ornamentation was damaged. The last major period of change

came in Victorian times, when many churches were 'restored'. Thatched naves were roofed in slate, old style box pews were replaced, and organs came into general use.

Many of Suffolk's most famous inhabitants have come from the arts - poets, painters, or musicians. George Crabbe is probably the county's most distinguished poet, who was born in Aldeburgh in 1754. His poem about the embittered fisherman Peter Grimes inspired an opera by a much later and better known resident, Benjamin Britten.

The first Aldeburgh Festival came about in 1948, founded by Britten, the singer Peter Pears, and Eric Crozier. They decided to set up a modest festival, initially held in Aldeburgh's Jubilee Hall, and various churches in the area. The festival's popularity grew to the point where a permanent home for the festival was founded at Snape Maltings.

It was Aldeburgh, too, that was home to Elizabeth Garrett Anderson, the first woman Doctor of Medicine, and founder of a hospital in London. She also became the first woman mayor of an English Borough when she took up office in Aldeburgh in 1908. Thomas Gainsborough worked in Bath, and later London, but it was in Suffolk where he was born and brought up. The house in Sudbury where Gainsborough was born, formerly a 16th century inn, is now preserved as a museum and exhibition gallery, and it is the only artist's birthplace open to the public in the country. While Gainsborough loved to paint landscapes, it was the informality and grace of his portraits which won him far-reaching acclaim.

But of course Suffolk's best known painter is also one of Britain's - John Constable, who was born in 1776. His father, Golding, a miller, owned mills at Dedham and Flatford, and two windmills at East Bergholt. Golding wanted him to follow in the family business, but with encouragement from his mother, John went to London to study art, eventually gaining a place at the Royal Academy. Although his early commissions were not to his own taste, he persevered with painting the countryside where he was brought up around Dedham Vale, in a style which at the time was not generally acceptable. When 'The Hay Wain' was first shown in the Royal Academy in 1818, it received a response which was lukewarm, to say the least. In Paris, where impressionist painting had already taken off, he was feted as a celebrity, and was awarded a gold medal by the King of France. His work only received recognition at home later on.

SOMERLEYTON HALL 1891 28725

Somerleyton Hall dates back to Elizabethan times, although it was extensively rebuilt in 1846 by Sir Samuel Morton Peto, who made his fortune out of the railways. The mansion has some lavishly furnished state rooms, and the gardens include a maze.

SOMERLEYTON HALL 1891 28730

Somerleyton Hall's impressive cast iron and glass-domed winter garden, with its rich abundance of ferns, climbing plants and typical Victorian ornamentation. It was demolished in 1914.

LOWESTOFT
Entrance to the Harbour **1887**
A sailing vessel negotiates the harbour entrance. This is where busy port and tourism came together. The South Pier, which forms the southern part of the harbour, and from where this picture was taken, was a popular stroll for holidaymakers.

LOWESTOFT
The Beach 1887
A typical late Victorian beach scene, with donkey rides, a complete absence of skin exposed to the sun, and a photographer's equipment - a tripod and a cart for storing the glass plates - to the left of the picture.

LOWESTOFT, ENTRANCE TO THE HARBOUR 1887   19838

LOWESTOFT, THE BEACH 1887   19886

Lowestoft
Convalescent Home 1887 19856

**LOWESTOFT,
LONDON ROAD 1896** 37924
Here we see solid Victorian
architecture in this tree-lined
street, with one well-established
family retail chain much in
evidence. Lowestoft is very
much a mixture of fishing port
and seaside resort, the latter
the result of the arrival of the
railway in the mid
19th century.

LOWESTOFT, SOUTH PIER PAVILION 1896 37937a
The South Pier was built to shelter Lowestoft's outer harbour in the mid-19th century by Samuel Morton Peto.
At the time of this photograph, the iron-framed Pier Pavilion had been open for five years. It survived until after
World War II.

LOWESTOFT
The Yacht Basin 1896

The iron-framed Pier Pavilion can be seen in the background. The growth of Lowestoft in Victorian times was largely down to construction by the civil engineer Samuel Morton Peto, who lived in the splendid Somerleyton Hall nearby. He was also involved with the building of Nelson's Column, the Houses of Parliament, and railway lines the world over.

◆

LOWESTOFT
The High Lighthouse 1921

The changeover from sail to steam saw a resurgence in business for the port of Lowestoft. This photograph of the High Lighthouse was taken at a time when the Great War, which saw the use of tanks like this one, was still very much in recent memory.

LOWESTOFT, THE YACHT BASIN 1896   37939

LOWESTOFT, THE HIGH LIGHTHOUSE 1921   71705

LOWESTOFT, THE SEA FRONT 1922 72505a
Holidaymakers enjoy a bracing walk as the waves crash up against the sea wall. From the amount of spray being kicked up in the distance, it's a fair bet that somebody got wet!

COVEHITHE, THE CHURCH AND RUINS 1892 29930
This is St Andrews church and the ruins of the former nave. The original church was left in ruins after the Civil War, and the smaller replacement was built within the ruins, its tower a useful navigational aid for mariners offshore. The ruins were the subject of a watercolour by the artist John Sell Cotman in 1804.

HALESWORTH, MARKET PLACE c1955 H384019
Just north of the village is Brewery House, home of Sir William Hooker and his son Joseph. Not satisfied with the family business of brewing, they left to travel the world collecting plants, and eventually founded Kew Gardens.

**HALESWORTH,
THE THOROUGHFARE c1955**
H384005
The Thoroughfare is
Halesworth's main shopping
street. In the mid 18th
century, improvements in
navigation on the River Blyth
led to a big improvement in
trade for the area's maltsters
and brewers.

BLYTHBURGH, THE CHURCH 1895 36879

BLYTHBURGH
The Church 1895

Blythburgh was an important port in bygone times. In the same way as many other river ports, it lost trade when its waterways could no longer cope with the increasing draughts of cargo ships. The church, known locally as 'the cathedral of the marshes', with its 128ft nave and 83ft tower, presents an imposing landmark. It was over this church that a Liberator bomber exploded in August 1944, killing Joseph Kennedy, eldest brother of the late US president.

SOUTHWOLD
High Street 1892

Broad pavements and a dirt road characterise this turn-of-the-century view. These days, the renowned Crown Hotel presents less of a stark exterior, with a lighter colour scheme, and potted plants and shrubs.

SOUTHWOLD, HIGH STREET 1892 29926

SOUTHWOLD 1893 32182

Close to the point where the cliffs begin to rise from the beach at Southwold is the Sailor's Reading Room. It was founded in 1864 by a naval widow, whose intentions were 'to wean the fishermen from their alleged failings - going to sea on the Sabbath, and getting drunk on any day of the week'. The beach itself is dotted with numerous fishing boats.

SOUTHWOLD, EAST GREEN 1893 32184

Looming over the rooftops is the gleaming white tower of the lighthouse, built just six years previously. These days, East Green is perhaps best known as the Mecca for all local beer drinkers - Adnams Brewery!

SOUTHWOLD, GENERAL VIEW 1893 32186
While many houses burned down in the fire of 1659, the 15th century church of St. Edmund survived because the churchyard served as a fire break.

SOUTHWOLD, THE BEACH 1896 38620
The beach is lined with numerous beach yawls; these did all the fetching and carrying for the cargo-carrying ships which plied the North Sea, as well as competing for lucrative salvage prizes when they foundered. Double-ended clinker-built boats with twin lugsails, they were capable of sailing at speed, an essential prerequisite for the job.

SOUTHWOLD
The Green 1896

In 1659, Southwold suffered a huge fire which destroyed a substantial part of the town. The rebuilding which followed left nine greens - effective firebreaks against any future catastrophe - and it is these which give Southwold its unique character.

SOUTHWOLD
The Common 1899

Cows graze on Southwold's Common. In the distance is the church of St Edmund, built in the mid 15th century, and one of the few buildings in Southwold which survived the fire of 1659.

SOUTHWOLD, THE GREEN 1896 38624

SOUTHWOLD, THE COMMON 1899 44502

SOUTHWOLD, THE MARKET 1896 38627
It must have been a hot day when this
photograph was taken - note the
boaters, the parasol and the baby in a
frilly sunbonnet enjoying a ride in a
goatcart. The market still takes place
here today.

SOUTHWOLD, FROM THE PIER 1906 56829a
A typical beach scene, in an age when modesty was paramount. Ladies would take to the water from the bathing machines rolled down to water's edge. The holidaymakers in the deck chairs on the beach will be 'taking the air' rather than working on suntans - a tanned skin would not become fashionable until the 1920s.

SOUTHWOLD, MARKET PLACE 1919 69121
The centre of the Market Place is marked by a splendid Victorian cast iron water pump, decorated with fish, crown and arrows, and the motto 'Defend They Ryghts'. The Swan Hotel is mainly Georgian, with Edwardian bays added on. Note the elegant wrought ironwork above the sign.

WALBERSWICK, THE RIVER BANK 1892 29933
This couple passing the time of day, or maybe waiting for the ferry to take them across the river to Southwold, are on the bank of the River Blyth.

WALBERSWICK, THE FERRY 1919 69127
This chain ferry across the River Blyth from Walberswick to Southwold was operated by the River Blyth Ferry Company. Started up in 1885, the original hand-cranked ferry was later replaced by one which was steam-powered.

WALBERSWICK, THE BRIDGE 1919 69129
A quaint wooden footbridge gives this pedestrian relatively quick access over the River Blyth where it is joined by Buss Creek to Southwold . Horsedrawn carriages and motorised vehicles had to take a much longer route, about nine miles, via Blythburgh.

WALBERSWICK, THE VILLAGE 1919 69128a
The village green is overlooked by the Bell Inn. Just beyond the Inn is an area known as the 'fishermen's flats' (these days a car park), where the fishermen laid out their nets on trestles to dry.

DUNWICH, THE VILLAGE 1909 62043

DUNWICH
The Village 1909
Not much more than St James's Street is left of Dunwich, once the seat of the Saxon king of East Anglia, and once one of the greatest and most prosperous ports in the country. When this picture was taken, what remained of Dunwich still had the last of its old churches. It had started to collapse five years previously, and finally fell into the sea in 1918.

◆

YOXFORD
The Village 1909
North of Saxmundham, Yoxford was once a coaching stop on the London to Great Yarmouth route. Outside St Peter's church, an ornate cast iron signpost erected in 1830 has hands pointing to London, Yarmouth and Framlingham. The business of taking a photograph is still sufficiently unusual to ensure the subjects do not act naturally, and inevitably one of the boys has failed to heed the photographer's pleas to keep still for the duration of the exposure!

YOXFORD, THE VILLAGE 1909 62051

SAXMUNDHAM 1929 82948a

SAXMUNDHAM, HIGH STREET 1929
82947
Saxmundham saw a good deal of
change when the railway arrived in
the 19th century. The Bell Hotel
was built in 1842.

LEISTON, SIZEWELL ROAD 1922 72579
There's a delightfully pensive look on the face of the little girl in this picture. Did the photographer capture a genuine moment, or was she posed? On the other side of the street, well-known shoe retailers Freeman, Hardy and Willis announce the best bargains since the beginning of the Great War.

LEISTON, THE ABBEY 1894 33370

North of Leiston are the flint and brick ruins of the 14th-century Leiston Abbey. Of the church, only the Lady Chapel remains as a complete building, a result of its usefulness for storing grain after the Dissolution.

LEISTON, HIGH STREET 1922 72577

The headline on the newsagent's billboard refers to the continuing turmoil that followed the end of World War I and the Treaty of Versailles, and the Germans' obligation to pay reparations.

LEISTON
The Abbey 1922

Founded in 1182, it was not until a couple of hundred years later that the abbey really made its mark when a group of Premonstratensian Canons moved here from nearby Minsmere. They brought all the Norman masonry from their original abbey and reused it here.

◆

THORPENESS
The Boat House 1922

The Boat House on the right of this view was one of the earliest buildings of Glencairn Stuart Ogilvie's holiday village to be completed in 1911, even before the Meare itself was finished. Light snacks and afternoon teas were served here, giving visitors something pleasant to round off their day's boating.

LEISTON, THE ABBEY 1922 72584

THORPENESS, THE BOAT HOUSE 1922 72589

THORPENESS, THE LAKE 1922 72591

The Meare was a three feet deep lake, actually formed by accident when the Hundred River flooded. Estate owner Glencairn Stuart Ogilvie decided to keep it, building his holiday village around it.

THORPENESS 1929 82979

Here we are overlooking the beach, the upper part populated by marram or 'bentgrass'. As a holiday village, what we see here has to be one of the first examples of parking problems anywhere!

THORPENESS, THE HOUSE IN THE CLOUDS AND THE MILL c1955 T38012a

The curious 'House in the Clouds' is in fact a water tower. The upper part conceals the tank, while the creosoted portion below provides living accommodation. The post mill in the foreground originally ground corn at Aldringham, but was moved to its present position in the 1920s to pump water into the 'House in the Clouds'.

SNAPE, THE CHURCH 1909 62024

In 1862, an important archaeological find was made half a mile east from here. A Saxon ship burial was discovered, 48 feet long. It has since been dated to between AD635 and 650.

ALDEBURGH, THE ESPLANADE 1894 33355

This view looks south from one of the two lookout towers on the beach. The yawls parked on the beach were organised into two companies, the 'Up-towners' and 'Down-towners', with their respective headquarters at the lookout towers. Intermingled with the boats are bathing machines, evidence of Aldeburgh's growing tourist industry.

ALDEBURGH
The Moot Hall 1894
The timber-framed Tudor Moot Hall is situated next to the beach. When it was built, the meeting house was actually right in the centre of town, but coastal erosion over hundreds of years has swept away much of the old town, and left the beach almost next door to the building.

◆

ALDEBURGH
The Esplanade 1896
Holidaymakers enjoy a stroll along the Parade. In the distance is a lookout tower, one of two. While there are recreational activities available on the beach, it is very much a working one, evidenced by the yawls on the shingle.

ALDEBURGH, THE MOOT HALL 1894 33360

ALDEBURGH, THE ESPLANADE 1896 38668

ALDEBURGH, THE LIFEBOAT 'WINCHESTER' 1903 50426
While most people imagine lifeboats generally to be launched from slipways, Aldeburgh lifeboats such as the 'Winchester' have always been launched straight from the shingle beach. Four years earlier, an Aldeburgh lifeboat suffered its worst disaster, capsizing with the loss of seven lives.

ALDEBURGH, THE BEACH 1906 56817
The ever-changing coastline has very much dictated the fortunes of Aldeburgh, but one thing which has not changed is the activity of local fishermen, who park their boats on the shingle bank which runs along the beach. Here, Edwardian bathers are braving the chilly East coast waters.

ALDEBURGH, THE MOOT HALL 1906 56822
Here we see the Moot Hall from the beach. The building was once in the centre of a much larger town, but coastal erosion saw much of Aldeburgh lost to the sea.

ALDEBURGH, THE STEPS 1906 56826
The High Street is Aldeburgh's main area of activity, and from here the Town Steps lead off up a steep hill. Here grand houses enjoy a superb view overlooking the town and coastline below.

ALDEBURGH, OLD MARKET SQUARE 1929

82976

The poet George Crabbe was born in
Aldeburgh in 1754. His poem about the
embittered fisherman Peter Grimes
inspired an opera by a much later and
better known resident, Benjamin Britten.
Just 14 years after this photograph was
taken, Elizabeth Garrett Anderson, the first
woman Doctor of Medicine, became first
woman mayor of an English borough when
she took up office in Aldeburgh in 1908.

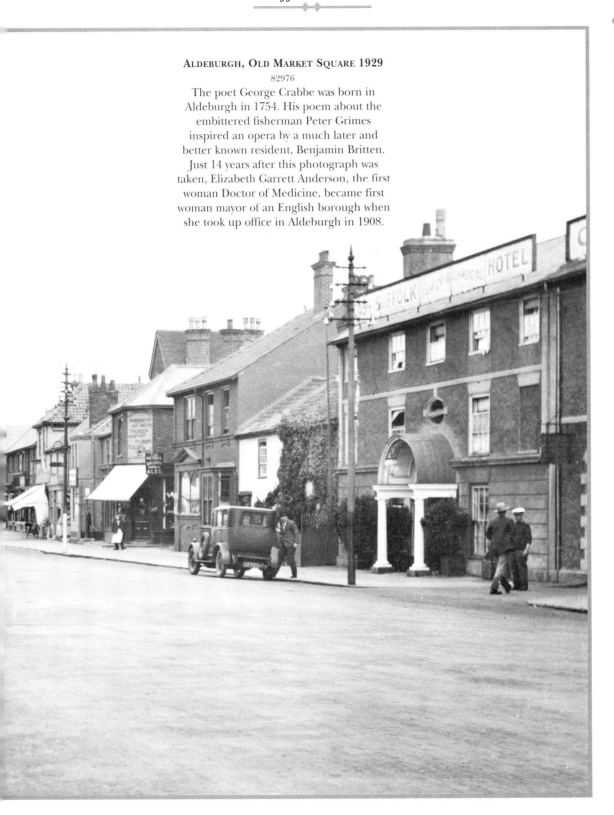

ALDEBURGH, THE MILL HOUSE 1909 62012

ALDEBURGH
The Mill House 1909
The tongues must have wagged when
the first residents moved into the Mill
House on Crags Path. It had been
converted into living accommodation
seven years previously by a monk who
renounced his holy orders to take a
Scandinavian wife!

ALDEBURGH
High Street 1894
The broad High Street is mainly
Victorian, peppered with Georgian
buildings. The original Tudor town plan
was based on a series of both parallel
and converging streets, but erosion
during the 17th and 18th centuries
resulted in many houses being lost
to the sea.

ALDEBURGH, HIGH STREET 1894 33362

BAWDSEY, DISTANT VIEW OF BAWDSEY MANOR 1894 34806

Looking across the River Deben , with a distant Bawdsey Manor on the far shore. This late Victorian manor later played a vital role during the Second World War as a radar station warning of impending German air raids.

BAWDSEY , THE VILLAGE GREEN 1907 58988

A tranquil scene in the quiet little village of Bawdsey. Some thirty years later, Bawdsey was to play a vital part in the defence of Britain against the Luftwaffe. This is where the scientist Robert Watson-Watt developed radar, and indeed, here too was one of the five strategic radar stations situated along the coast between Bawdsey and Dover.

ORFORD, THE VILLAGE 1909 62017
Henry II's great 12th-century keep stands sentinel over Orford, built to guard the coast where Flemish mercenaries were brought ashore by the Earl of Norfolk, whose castles far out-numbered royal castles in East Anglia. It was the first to be built with a keep which is cylindrical inside and polygonal outside, reinforced by three projecting rectangular turrets.

ORFORD, THE QUAY 1937 88246
In the far distance, across the river, are some of the defence installations built on Orford Ness during World War I. During World War II, Orford Ness was used by the scientist Robert Watson-Watt to develop radar.

ORFORD, THE VILLAGE c1955 O20065

The tower of St Bartholomew's church dominates this view of Orford. The upper part of the tower collapsed in 1830, and it was not until the early 1960s that reconstruction began, ending in 1971.

WOODBRIDGE, THE BELL INN 1894 33375

The Bell Inn (now the Bell and Steelyard) stands in New Street. The covered hoist is a steelyard, used for weighing grain wagons from the early 17th century to the 1880s. Capable of weighing up to 2.5 tons, it would weigh the wagon before going to market, and again when it returned empty. No doubt the day's trade would be celebrated over a pint in the inn!

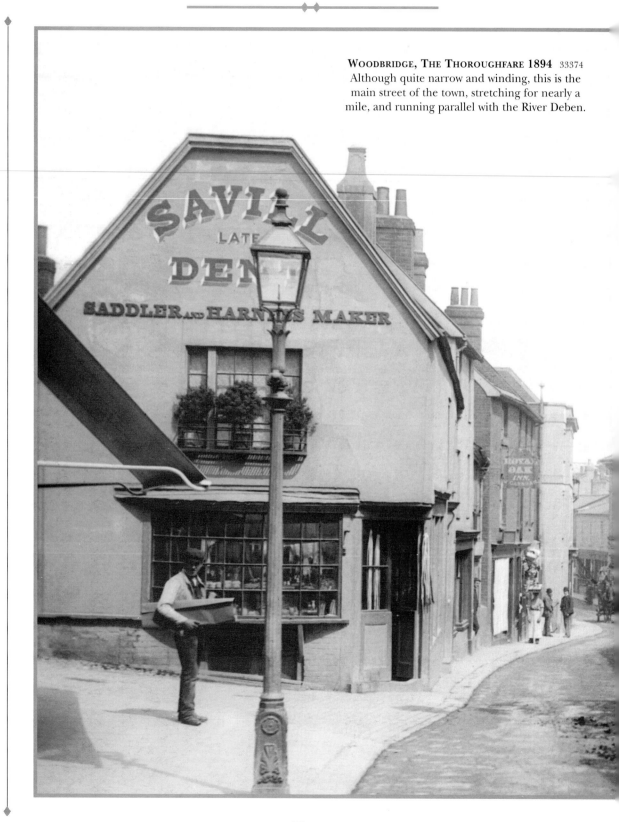

WOODBRIDGE, THE THOROUGHFARE 1894 33374
Although quite narrow and winding, this is the main street of the town, stretching for nearly a mile, and running parallel with the River Deben.

WOODBRIDGE, FROM THE CHURCH TOWER 1894 33984

At the bottom of the picture is the Bull Hotel, host to Alfred Lord Tennyson in 1876, when he was Poet Laureate. Another well-known poet lived nearby - Edward Fitzgerald, who translated the Rubaiyat of Omar Khayyam.

WOODBRIDGE, CHURCH STREET 1906 53497

This view looks along Church Street at its junction with Cumberland Street (left) and the Thoroughfare (right). The Cross Public House, according to its sign established in 1652, almost certainly took its name from its position on the crossroads.

WOODBRIDGE, THE TOWN HALL 1908 60685

Built in 1575 by Thomas Seckford, Elizabeth I's Master of the Rolls, Woodbridge's Shire Hall stands on an island in the middle of Market Hill. The Dutch gables and double staircase leading to the upper rooms were added in the early 18th century.

WOODBRIDGE, THE PROMENADE 1906 53495

The bank of the river Deben. Just to the right of the sailing barge is Woodbridge tide mill, the later model of a tide mill which has stood here since the early 12th century.

WOODBRIDGE
THE BEACH 1898 42772

**FELIXSTOWE,
FROM THE BEACH 1899** 44513
No shortage of holidaymakers on
the beach at turn-of-the-century
Felixstowe. The only shortage here,
a hundred years ago, is that of
exposed skin. This was an era when
modesty prevailed.

FELIXSTOWE, THE BEACH 1899 44516a
A crowded beach, with little more than a few square inches of skin exposed to the sun. At the end of Victoria's reign, remaining fully clothed and using parasols to protect against the sun was very much the order of the day for relaxation on the beach.

FELIXSTOWE, STREET SCENE 1899 44519
Capturing a street scene on film was not as easy a hundred years ago as it is now. But despite the fact that the relatively long exposure has meant that the moving people have blurred, the resulting photograph conveys a natural feel that is lacking in so many posed scenes of the same era.

WALTON, HIGH STREET 1899 43246
At this time, Felixstowe enjoyed popularity as a seaside resort, but the dream of eccentric local landowner Colonel Tomline to transform the town into a major port had not yet materialised - that was to take another fifty years! Here, in Walton High Street, the occasional pony and trap seems to be the only contribution to heavy traffic.

FELIXSTOWE, THE BEACH 1904 51254

At the turn of the century, Felixstowe was at the height of its popularity as a seaside resort, with its south-facing beach. Of course, in Edwardian times bathing machines were very much the order of the day, and even on the beach a strict sense of decorum was maintained.

FELIXSTOWE, THE PIER 1906 54640

At this time, Felixstowe was a genteel seaside resort, with steamers pulling up at the pier with passengers from Great Yarmouth, Walton-on-the-Naze, Clacton, and even London. Perhaps the most interesting thing about this photograph is the parked car on the right. Closer examination reveals that in fact the car was pasted over the original print - common practice at the time to bring photographs up to date.

FELIXSTOWE
The Gardens and Cliff Hotel 1907
There is a strong sense of the unnatural in this picture. Outside the very grand Cliff Hotel, these subjects are all quite clearly posing for the photographer, and not making a very convincing job of it - even those virtually out of shot!

◆

FELIXSTOWE 1907
At this time, seaside entertainment at Felixstowe had not progressed to the garishly commercialised pursuits of today. Donkey rides were a traditional favourite, along with rides in carriages pulled by goats.

FELIXSTOWE, THE GARDENS AND CLIFF HOTEL 1907 58965

FELIXSTOWE 1907 58978

FELIXSTOWE, THE DOCKS 1907 58986

It was local landowner Colonel Tomline who promoted a railway and a new dock in Felixstowe, in the hope of being able to compete with the port of Harwich across the Orwell Estuary. The dock did not succeed until well after his death, but the railway meantime stimulated the development of Felixstowe as a seaside resort.

FELIXSTOWE, THE SPA PAVILION 1909 62005

When the railway arrived in 1877, it did not just create Felixstowe as a place for seaside trippers. The spa and gardens made it far more genteel and upmarket. It even catered for the Empress of Germany, who came here in 1891. Forty-five years later, Mrs Wallis Simpson was resident in Felixstowe during the abdication crisis.

PIN MILL 1909 62001a
Probably the most well known pub on the East Coast, the Butt and Oyster at Pin Mill, on the River Orwell.
Across the river from here is Orwell Park; in the 18th century it was the home of 'Old Grog' - Admiral Vernon.
It was he who won sailors their daily ration of grog - rum and water.

BECCLES, THE RIVER BRIDGE 1894 33331a
The 97 feet high tower of St Michael's church dominates this view of Beccles, seen from the River Waveney.
Wherries were still used to transport heavy goods, such as the timber seen here.

BECCLES, FROM THE MARSHES 1894 33332

This view is from the marsh-lined River Waveney. In the days when trading wherries plied their way up and down the rivers, transporting goods from the East Coast sea ports, or from one town to another, Beccles was a thriving port.

BECCLES, MARKET SQUARE 1900 45096

The Market Square of Beccles is overlooked by the detached tower of St Michael's church. The building on the left was home to the offices of the East Suffolk Gazette, with the ground floor taken up as a shop.

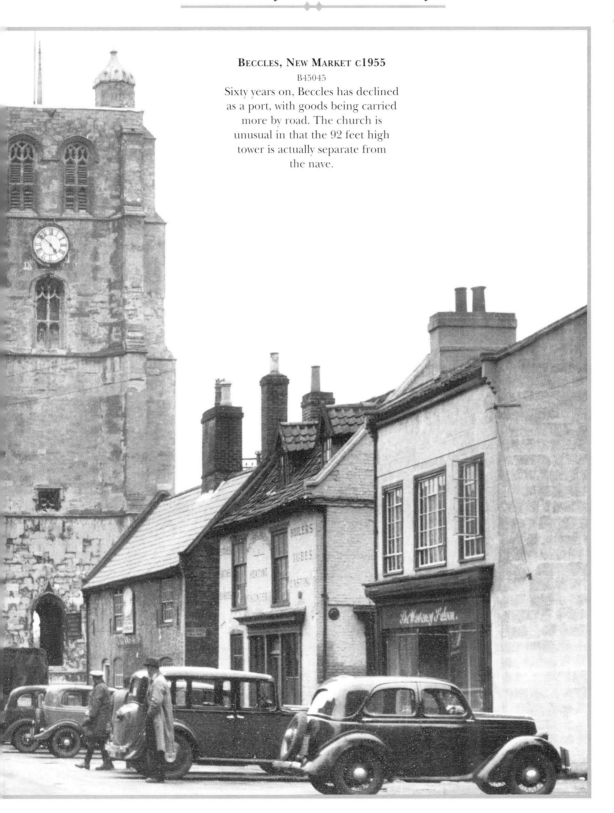

BECCLES, NEW MARKET C1955

B45045

Sixty years on, Beccles has declined as a port, with goods being carried more by road. The church is unusual in that the 92 feet high tower is actually separate from the nave.

BUNGAY, RIVER WAVENEY c1955 B617002

In the days when Bungay was a thriving port, trading wherries would come through Geldeston Lock near Beccles, and sail up the Waveney to what used to be the limit of navigation for large craft. Later on, the Waveney became limited to small pleasure boats, such as this rowing boat seen on a tranquil stretch of the river.

BUNGAY, MARKET PLACE 1951 B617026

A year after a fire razed most of Bungay to the ground in 1688, the Butter Cross was built to commemorate it. It is a pretty octagonal building with a dome surmounted by a figure of Justice; a cage underneath was used to hold the local felons to public ridicule, although by the time this photograph was taken, it was no longer in service! The board standing up against one of the pillars is offering a circular tour of Southwold and Lowestoft.

BUNGAY
The Castle c1965

Bungay was one of the seats of the powerful Bigod family, who built the castle here in 1170, making use of a loop in the River Waveney to provide a natural defence. When it fell into disuse, as with so many such buildings, the locals made good use of it as an abundant supply of building material.

◆

BRANDON
The River Ouse 1925

Tables and chairs are ready in a relaxing riverside setting. Barges once travelled up the Little Ouse as far as Brandon and Thetford, although here it is much more the province of pleasure boaters.

BUNGAY, THE CASTLE c1965 B617053

BRANDON, THE RIVER OUSE 1925 78270

BRANDON, HIGH STREET 1925 78266a

BRANDON, MARKET PLACE 1925 78271a
Brandon's market has been in existence for over 650 years. The town was once the centre of flint-knapping, at its height during the Napoleonic wars, employing two hundred men producing gunflints.

IPSWICH, THE BUTTER MARKET 1893
32204
On the corner with St Stephens Lane stands the Ancient House, a remarkable building which is probably the best surviving example of medieval pargetting - decorative plasterwork - in Britain.

IPSWICH, THE ANCIENT HOUSE 1893 32205
When this photograph was taken, the richly pargetted Ancient House, which dates back to medieval times, was occupied by Fred Pawsey, selling books and stationery.

IPSWICH, THE DOCKS 1893 32208
Ipswich, at the head of the Orwell Estuary, has been a major port for centuries. When this picture was taken, the port was starting to enjoy commercial success after a long period of decline.

IPSWICH, ST STEPHENS LANE 1921 70391
It is three years after World War I, and a packet of ten Wills cigarettes can be bought in this tobacconists for 3d (three old pence). The newspapers are full of the news of the impending strike by the miners. Prime Minister Lloyd George had strikes by the miners, railwaymen and many others broken by troops and the use of emergency powers.

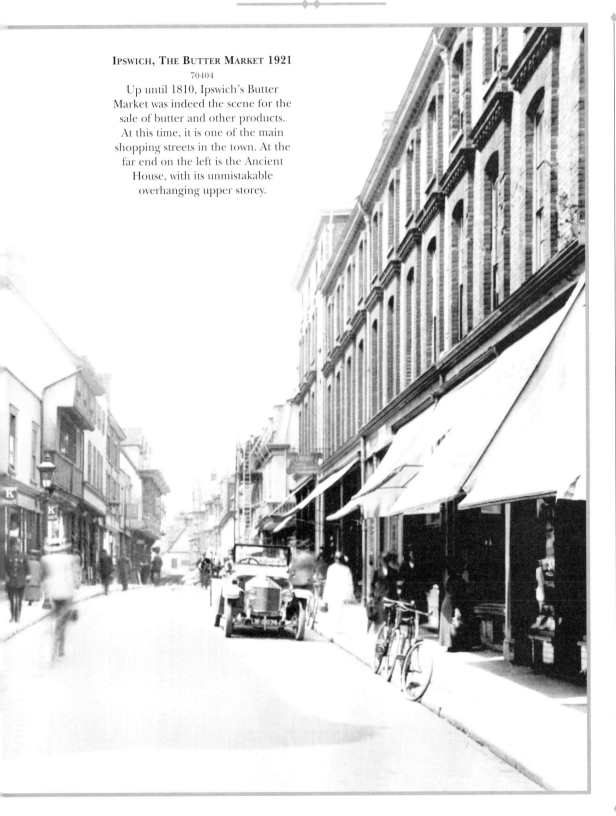

IPSWICH, THE BUTTER MARKET 1921

70404

Up until 1810, Ipswich's Butter Market was indeed the scene for the sale of butter and other products. At this time, it is one of the main shopping streets in the town. At the far end on the left is the Ancient House, with its unmistakable overhanging upper storey.

IPSWICH, THE ANCIENT HOUSE 1921 70399

IPSWICH
The Ancient House 1921
Without doubt the best known building in Ipswich, the Ancient House (or Sparrowe's House) with its incredible plasterwork. It was around 1670 that Robert Sparrowe remodelled the building, with the pargetting reflecting his interest in the known world at that time - the four continents of Europe, Africa, Asia and America.

IPSWICH
The Lock Gates 1921
A sailing barge negotiates the lock gates. The Wet Dock was constructed in Ipswich between 1839 and 1842, and at the time it was the most revolutionary and the biggest of its kind in the country.

IPSWICH, THE LOCK GATES 1921 70413

IPSWICH, ST PETERS DOCK 1921 70411a
Sailing barges tied up in the Wet Dock, the non-tidal part of the port of Ipswich. Adjacent to the dock are large warehouses, including that of Cranfields, who along with Pauls, owned their own large fleets of barges.

IPSWICH, THE RIVER ORWELL 1921 70414

A sailing barge makes its way past a moored steamer. Outside the Wet Dock, tidal moorings were built for larger ships.

FRAMLINGHAM, THE CASTLE 1909 62032

The castle was built in 1190 by the famous Bigod family, and was one of the first castles not to include a keep. Instead, it has thirteen separate towers, linked by a curtain wall, a Saracen idea brought back by returning Crusaders. It was at Framlingham in 1553 that Mary Tudor organised her army of supporters to march on Lady Jane Grey, and here, later, she proclaimed herself Queen.

FRAMLINGHAM
Market Hill 1929

Although best known for its castle, Framlingham's heart is Market Hill, in a town where many of the buildings are in fact made from stones removed from the castle. Nearby, the early 18th century Unitarian chapel retains doors which segregate the sexes.

◆

BILDESTON
The Square c1960

The war memorial, clock tower and telephone box grace the Square. In the church nearby is a memorial to Captain Edward Rotherham, who commanded a ship of the line, the 'Royal Sovereign', at the Battle of Trafalgar.

FRAMLINGHAM, MARKET HILL 1929 82062

BILDESTON, THE SQUARE C1960 B766021

HADLEIGH, OLD HOUSES IN THE HIGH STREET, 1922 71970

HADLEIGH, THE DEANERY TOWER 1922 71976

HADLEIGH
Old Houses in the High Street, 1922
These are 17th-century buildings. The Coffee Tavern came into being around thirty years previously - in an attempt to provide people with an alternative to nearby public houses.

◆

HADLEIGH
The Deanery Tower 1922
When the Deanery Tower was built in the latter part of the 15th century by Suffolk's Archdeacon William Pykenham, it was supposed that it would be the gateway to a palace. But Pykenham's death put paid to further building. It is nevertheless a fine example of 15th-century brickwork.

HADLEIGH, HIGH STREET c1955 H2007

Looking in the opposite direction from the Coffee Tavern, this view of Hadleigh's High Street shows the George public house and, further down on the same side, the White Lion Hotel. The building in between has its upper storey decorated by pargetting - moulded plasterwork.

HADLEIGH, CHURCH STREET c1950 H2008

The church, one of the largest in Suffolk, is not a typical Suffolk wool church, and has an elegant lead spire. Inside, the 600-year-old Angelus Bell, one of the oldest in the country, is inscribed: Ave Maria Gracia Plena Dominus Tecum. Perhaps the man who made the bell had other things on his mind when it came to putting in the inscription, as he forgot to invert the words laterally in the mould, and they appear backwards on the finished article!

NEEDHAM MARKET, HIGH STREET 1922 71933a
In the distance is the church of St John the Baptist, once a chapel to nearby Barking. From the outside, the roof has an odd look about it, but inside, it is one of the most remarkable examples of a timber roof in East Anglia.

NEEDHAM MARKET
Hawks Mill c1955
The imposing brick-built Victorian Hawks Mill astride the River Gipping. In recent years, the building has been converted into living accommodation.

OLD NEWTON
The School c1955
The village school in Old Newton, just north of Stowmarket. This was an era when every village had its school - now of course, much consolidation has taken place.

NEEDHAM MARKET, HAWKS MILL c1955 N155027

OLD NEWTON, THE SCHOOL c1955 O97013

STOWMARKET, IPSWICH STREET c1955 S583007a

When this photograph was taken, Ipswich Street in Stowmarket was part of the main road between Ipswich and Bury St Edmunds. From the amount of traffic here, it is hard to imagine that it became so heavy that the town now has a bypass.

WICKHAM MARKET
Market Hill & Middle Hill 1929
This quiet little village north of Woodbridge was granted a market in the mid 15th century by Henry VI. Four hundred years later, it was here that John Kirby wrote his influential 'Suffolk Traveller'.

WICKHAM MARKET, MARKET HILL 1929 82047

WICKHAM MARKET, MIDDLE HILL 1929 82051

FLATFORD, BRIDGE COTTAGE 1907 57552

FLATFORD
Bridge Cottage 1907
It was Flatford and nearby East Bergholt which provided the young John Constable with the inspiration for many of his fine paintings. Flatford Mill, built in 1733, featured in several of Constable's works. This thatched cottage is called, appropriately enough, Bridge Cottage.

FLATFORD
Willy Lott's Cottage 1907
Beside the quiet mill-pond at Flatford Mill stands Willy Lott's Cottage, instantly recognisable as the setting for Constable's famous painting 'The Hay Wain'. Willy Lott, the mill-hand, is reputed to have lived in this cottage for eighty-eight years.

FLATFORD, WILLY LOTT'S COTTAGE 1907 57554

LAVENHAM, THE GUILDHALL 1904 51180

This early 16th-century timber building was commissioned by the Guild of Corpus Christi, a trade organisation which regulated the local industry of wool production. The heavy oak studwork - far more than is required for structural stability - reflects the wealth of the wool trade.

MONK'S ELEIGH, THE STREET c1955 M270003

Thatched roofs abound. While wheat straw is often used as the roofing material, the chances are that these houses will be thatched with longer-lasting reed from the Broads. The church and green were once the subject of railway posters promoting Suffolk.

LONG MELFORD, MELFORD HALL 1895 35492

Melford Hall is a Tudor turreted brick mansion. Its bricks were supposedly made from clay dug out of the Green, and the hall was originally used by the Abbots of Bury St Edmunds as a hunting lodge. The children's writer and illustrator Beatrix Potter spent many happy holidays here with her cousin, Lady Hyde Parker.

LONG MELFORD, KENTWELL HALL 1895 35495

The red-brick Tudor manor house of Kentwell Hall stands at the northern end of Long Melford. Today it is best known for the striking Tudor Rose brickwork maze set into the courtyard.

SUDBURY, NORTH STREET 1895 35469

SUDBURY, THE MILL 1895 35484
The Town Mill was built on the site of a Saxon mill. The youths sitting on the wall in front could be posing for the camera, or they might just be dangling a line into the mill stream to see what they might catch. In recent years, the building has been converted into a hotel, with the water wheel inside kept as a feature of the dining room.

SUDBURY, THE MARKET 1904 51156
Market Hill is lined with elegant Georgian buildings, with St Peter's Church at the top. The artist Thomas Gainsborough was born here in a former 16th-century inn, and he lived and worked here for a number of years.

PAKENHAM, THE WINDMILL c1955 P286003

PAKENHAM
The Windmill c1955
The village of Pakenham is noted for having both a watermill and windmill in close proximity to each other. The tower windmill was built in 1831. Note the large millstones standing up against the tower on either side of the doorway.

BURY ST EDMUNDS
Arch of Norman Tower 1898
The Norman Gate was built by Abbot Anselm in the first half of the 12th century, providing an entrance gate to the impressive abbey church. After the abbey was destroyed, the tower was used as a bell tower for St James' Church, which, 16 years after this photograph was taken, became the cathedral for the diocese of St Edmundsbury and Ipswich.

BURY ST EDMUNDS, ARCH OF NORMAN TOWER 1898 41237

BURY ST EDMUNDS, THE ABBEY GATE 1922 71956a
This enormous gate, originally built with defence in mind, once led into the monastery courtyard. It stands on the site of an earlier gateway, which had been destroyed by the townsfolk during an uprising against the harsh rule of the Abbey.

BURY ST EDMUNDS, MARKET PLACE 1898

41246

The original market place, as laid out in the Bury St Edmunds' grid pattern devised by Abbot Baldwin in the 11th century, was a good deal larger than it was by the time this photograph was taken. Market stalls became permanent over the years, and ended up as two complete rows of buildings. Here, a few street vendors have set out their stalls.

BURY ST EDMUNDS, CROWN STREET 1929 81935

BURY ST EDMUNDS
Crown Street 1929
The 15th-century St Mary's church is the burial place of Mary Tudor, sister of Henry VIII, and noted for its decorated 'Angel Roof' nave. On the junction with Westgate Street is the Theatre Royal, one of only three surviving Regency theatres in the country, built in 1819 by National Gallery architect William Wilkins. The theatre is famous for its world premiere of 'Charley's Aunt' in 1892.

◆

BURY ST EDMUNDS
Churchgate Street 1929
When Abbot Anselm laid out his grid pattern for the streets of Bury St Edmunds, Churchgate Street was planned as the main thoroughfare, a ceremonial route to St Edmund's shrine.

BURY ST EDMUNDS, CHURCHGATE STREET 1929 81937

BURY ST EDMUNDS, ANGEL HOTEL 1929 81945
This photograph was taken back in the days when an open space in a town did not have to be completely covered by cars! The Angel Hotel was immortalised in Dickens' 'Pickwick Papers'.

BURY ST EDMUNDS, MARKET PLACE c1955 B258003
Angel Hill was once the site of Bury Fair, but by 1955 it has been relegated to nothing more than a car park. The Angel Hotel gave its name to the square.

BARTON MILLS, THE BULL INN 1925 78288

The pretty little village of Barton Mills, and the Bull Inn. In the 13th century, the local rector, Jacobus de Scabellis, became a cardinal, and ultimately, Pope Honorius IV.

MILDENHALL, HIGH STREET 1925 78279

Not something that would happen today with any degree of safety, a gentleman poses for the camera in the middle of the street. The timbered building on the left, occupied at the time by Barclays Bank, was originally built with plastered upper walls and gables, later exposed to give the building a mock Tudor flavour.

MILDENHALL
The War Memorial 1925
This photograph shows Mildenhall's war memorial, honouring the town's dead from the First World War. The statue is bright and new, and the grass is neatly trimmed.

MILDENHALL
Kingsway c1955
Thirty years can do a lot of damage, even to a statue. The statue is now discoloured, and the surrounding area overgrown.

MILDENHALL, THE WAR MEMORIAL 1925   78279A

MILDENHALL, KINGSWAY c1955   M75004

MILDENHALL, MARKET PLACE c1955 M75008

A small market town of medieval origin where the Fens meet Breckland, Mildenhall gained an airfield between the wars, the starting point for many famous air races. The airfield subsequently became a base for the United States Air Force (now the headquarters of the USAF in Europe). Here in the Market Place, the large car provides ample evidence of the American presence.

MILDENHALL, MARKET PLACE c1955 M75011

The 15th-century tower of St Mary's church overlooks the Market Place. The roof is decorated with angels bearing the marks of shots supposedly fired at them by Puritan soldiers. The spirelet on the corner of the tower was added in 1831.

MILDENHALL

MILDENHALL
High Street c1965

The church has a particularly fine ceiling decorated with angels. Just over twenty years previously, a farm worker had unearthed a hoard of Roman treasure - now displayed in the British Museum.

◆

NEWMARKET
High Street 1922

This photograph looks north along the High Street. As the main road from Norwich to London, it was a popular stopping off point for travellers in need of refreshment.

MILDENHALL, HIGH STREET C1965 M75056

NEWMARKET, HIGH STREET 1922 71914

NEWMARKET, HIGH STREET 1929 81955
The High Street used to be the main
Norwich to London road. Here is a
foretaste of the traffic problems that
were to come.

NEWMARKET, THE GRANDSTAND 1922 71932

Although the grandstand is strangely devoid of people and activity, this picture shows what Newmarket is all about: horse racing. Newmarket's connection with the sport dates back to the time of Charles II, although it was not until the reign of Victoria that horse racing received its biggest boost, promoted by her son the Prince of Wales.

NEWMARKET, HORSES AT EXERCISE 1922 71918

This is a daily sight around the capital of horse racing - stable lads exercising racehorses on Newmarket Heath.

NEWMARKET, THE CLOCK TOWER c1955   N23002
The clock tower at the northern end of the High Street was built to commemorate Queen Victoria's Golden
Jubilee in 1887. By the time this photograph was taken, it had been reduced to nothing more than an
ornamental roundabout for the traffic.

HAVERHILL, HIGH STREET c1955   H381003
The old part of the town is mainly late Victorian, although it expanded rapidly after World War II as an overspill
for London.

Index

Frith Book Co Titles

www.francisfrith.co.uk

The Frith Book Company publishes over 100 new titles each year. A selection of those currently available are listed below. For latest catalogue please contact Frith Book Co.

Town Books 96 pages, approx 100 photos. County and Themed Books 128 pages, approx 150 photos (unless specified). All titles hardback laminated case and jacket except those indicated pb (paperback)

Amersham, Chesham & Rickmansworth (pb)			Derby (pb)	1-85937-367-4	£9.99
	1-85937-340-2	£9.99	Derbyshire (pb)	1-85937-196-5	£9.99
Ancient Monuments & Stone Circles	1-85937-143-4	£17.99	Devon (pb)	1-85937-297-x	£9.99
Aylesbury (pb)	1-85937-227-9	£9.99	Dorset (pb)	1-85937-269-4	£9.99
Bakewell	1-85937-113-2	£12.99	Dorset Churches	1-85937-172-8	£17.99
Barnstaple (pb)	1-85937-300-3	£9.99	Dorset Coast (pb)	1-85937-299-6	£9.99
Bath (pb)	1-85937-419-0	£9.99	Dorset Living Memories	1-85937-210-4	£14.99
Bedford (pb)	1-85937-205-8	£9.99	Down the Severn	1-85937-118-3	£14.99
Berkshire (pb)	1-85937-191-4	£9.99	Down the Thames (pb)	1-85937-278-3	£9.99
Berkshire Churches	1-85937-170-1	£17.99	Down the Trent	1-85937-311-9	£14.99
Blackpool (pb)	1-85937-382-8	£9.99	Dublin (pb)	1-85937-231-7	£9.99
Bognor Regis (pb)	1-85937-431-x	£9.99	East Anglia (pb)	1-85937-265-1	£9.99
Bournemouth	1-85937-067-5	£12.99	East London	1-85937-080-2	£14.99
Bradford (pb)	1-85937-204-x	£9.99	East Sussex	1-85937-130-2	£14.99
Brighton & Hove(pb)	1-85937-192-2	£8.99	Eastbourne	1-85937-061-6	£12.99
Bristol (pb)	1-85937-264-3	£9.99	Edinburgh (pb)	1-85937-193-0	£8.99
British Life A Century Ago (pb)	1-85937-213-9	£9.99	England in the 1880s	1-85937-331-3	£17.99
Buckinghamshire (pb)	1-85937-200-7	£9.99	English Castles (pb)	1-85937-434-4	£9.99
Camberley (pb)	1-85937-222-8	£9.99	English Country Houses	1-85937-161-2	£17.99
Cambridge (pb)	1-85937-422-0	£9.99	Essex (pb)	1-85937-270-8	£9.99
Cambridgeshire (pb)	1-85937-420-4	£9.99	Exeter	1-85937-126-4	£12.99
Canals & Waterways (pb)	1-85937-291-0	£9.99	Exmoor	1-85937-132-9	£14.99
Canterbury Cathedral (pb)	1-85937-179-5	£9.99	Falmouth	1-85937-066-7	£12.99
Cardiff (pb)	1-85937-093-4	£9.99	Folkestone (pb)	1-85937-124-8	£9.99
Carmarthenshire	1-85937-216-3	£14.99	Glasgow (pb)	1-85937-190-6	£9.99
Chelmsford (pb)	1-85937-310-0	£9.99	Gloucestershire	1-85937-102-7	£14.99
Cheltenham (pb)	1-85937-095-0	£9.99	Great Yarmouth (pb)	1-85937-426-3	£9.99
Cheshire (pb)	1-85937-271-6	£9.99	Greater Manchester (pb)	1-85937-266-x	£9.99
Chester	1-85937-090-x	£12.99	Guildford (pb)	1-85937-410-7	£9.99
Chesterfield	1-85937-378-x	£9.99	Hampshire (pb)	1-85937-279-1	£9.99
Chichester (pb)	1-85937-228-7	£9.99	Hampshire Churches (pb)	1-85937-207-4	£9.99
Colchester (pb)	1-85937-188-4	£8.99	Harrogate	1-85937-423-9	£9.99
Cornish Coast	1-85937-163-9	£14.99	Hastings & Bexhill (pb)	1-85937-131-0	£9.99
Cornwall (pb)	1-85937-229-5	£9.99	Heart of Lancashire (pb)	1-85937-197-3	£9.99
Cornwall Living Memories	1-85937-248-1	£14.99	Helston (pb)	1-85937-214-7	£9.99
Cotswolds (pb)	1-85937-230-9	£9.99	Hereford (pb)	1-85937-175-2	£9.99
Cotswolds Living Memories	1-85937-255-4	£14.99	Herefordshire	1-85937-174-4	£14.99
County Durham	1-85937-123-x	£14.99	Hertfordshire (pb)	1-85937-247-3	£9.99
Croydon Living Memories	1-85937-162-0	£9.99	Horsham (pb)	1-85937-432-8	£9.99
Cumbria	1-85937-101-9	£14.99	Humberside	1-85937-215-5	£14.99
Dartmoor	1-85937-145-0	£14.99	Hythe, Romney Marsh & Ashford	1-85937-256-2	£9.99

Available from your local bookshop or from the publisher

Frith Book Co Titles (continued)

Title	ISBN	Price	Title	ISBN	Price
Ipswich (pb)	1-85937-424-7	£9.99	St Ives (pb)	1-85937415-8	£9.99
Ireland (pb)	1-85937-181-7	£9.99	Scotland (pb)	1-85937-182-5	£9.99
Isle of Man (pb)	1-85937-268-6	£9.99	Scottish Castles (pb)	1-85937-323-2	£9.99
Isles of Scilly	1-85937-136-1	£14.99	Sevenoaks & Tunbridge	1-85937-057-8	£12.99
Isle of Wight (pb)	1-85937-429-8	£9.99	Sheffield, South Yorks (pb)	1-85937-267-8	£9.99
Isle of Wight Living Memories	1-85937-304-6	£14.99	Shrewsbury (pb)	1-85937-325-9	£9.99
Kent (pb)	1-85937-189-2	£9.99	Shropshire (pb)	1-85937-326-7	£9.99
Kent Living Memories	1-85937-125-6	£14.99	Somerset	1-85937-153-1	£14.99
Lake District (pb)	1-85937-275-9	£9.99	South Devon Coast	1-85937-107-8	£14.99
Lancaster, Morecambe & Heysham (pb)	1-85937-233-3	£9.99	South Devon Living Memories	1-85937-168-x	£14.99
Leeds (pb)	1-85937-202-3	£9.99	South Hams	1-85937-220-1	£14.99
Leicester	1-85937-073-x	£12.99	Southampton (pb)	1-85937-427-1	£9.99
Leicestershire (pb)	1-85937-185-x	£9.99	Southport (pb)	1-85937-425-5	£9.99
Lincolnshire (pb)	1-85937-433-6	£9.99	Staffordshire	1-85937-047-0	£12.99
Liverpool & Merseyside (pb)	1-85937-234-1	£9.99	Stratford upon Avon	1-85937-098-5	£12.99
London (pb)	1-85937-183-3	£9.99	Suffolk (pb)	1-85937-221-x	£9.99
Ludlow (pb)	1-85937-176-0	£9.99	Suffolk Coast	1-85937-259-7	£14.99
Luton (pb)	1-85937-235-x	£9.99	Surrey (pb)	1-85937-240-6	£9.99
Maidstone	1-85937-056-x	£14.99	Sussex (pb)	1-85937-184-1	£9.99
Manchester (pb)	1-85937-198-1	£9.99	Swansea (pb)	1-85937-167-1	£9.99
Middlesex	1-85937-158-2	£14.99	Tees Valley & Cleveland	1-85937-211-2	£14.99
New Forest	1-85937-128-0	£14.99	Thanet (pb)	1-85937-116-7	£9.99
Newark (pb)	1-85937-366-6	£9.99	Tiverton (pb)	1-85937-178-7	£9.99
Newport, Wales (pb)	1-85937-258-9	£9.99	Torbay	1-85937-063-2	£12.99
Newquay (pb)	1-85937-421-2	£9.99	Truro	1-85937-147-7	£12.99
Norfolk (pb)	1-85937-195-7	£9.99	Victorian and Edwardian Cornwall	1-85937-252-x	£14.99
Norfolk Living Memories	1-85937-217-1	£14.99	Victorian & Edwardian Devon	1-85937-253-8	£14.99
Northamptonshire	1-85937-150-7	£14.99	Victorian & Edwardian Kent	1-85937-149-3	£14.99
Northumberland Tyne & Wear (pb)	1-85937-281-3	£9.99	Vic & Ed Maritime Album	1-85937-144-2	£17.99
North Devon Coast	1-85937-146-9	£14.99	Victorian and Edwardian Sussex	1-85937-157-4	£14.99
North Devon Living Memories	1-85937-261-9	£14.99	Victorian & Edwardian Yorkshire	1-85937-154-x	£14.99
North London	1-85937-206-6	£14.99	Victorian Seaside	1-85937-159-0	£17.99
North Wales (pb)	1-85937-298-8	£9.99	Villages of Devon (pb)	1-85937-293-7	£9.99
North Yorkshire (pb)	1-85937-236-8	£9.99	Villages of Kent (pb)	1-85937-294-5	£9.99
Norwich (pb)	1-85937-194-9	£8.99	Villages of Sussex (pb)	1-85937-295-3	£9.99
Nottingham (pb)	1-85937-324-0	£9.99	Warwickshire (pb)	1-85937-203-1	£9.99
Nottinghamshire (pb)	1-85937-187-6	£9.99	Welsh Castles (pb)	1-85937-322-4	£9.99
Oxford (pb)	1-85937-411-5	£9.99	West Midlands (pb)	1-85937-289-9	£9.99
Oxfordshire (pb)	1-85937-430-1	£9.99	West Sussex	1-85937-148-5	£14.99
Peak District (pb)	1-85937-280-5	£9.99	West Yorkshire (pb)	1-85937-201-5	£9.99
Penzance	1-85937-069-1	£12.99	Weymouth (pb)	1-85937-209-0	£9.99
Peterborough (pb)	1-85937-219-8	£9.99	Wiltshire (pb)	1-85937-277-5	£9.99
Piers	1-85937-237-6	£17.99	Wiltshire Churches (pb)	1-85937-171-x	£9.99
Plymouth	1-85937-119-1	£12.99	Wiltshire Living Memories	1-85937-245-7	£14.99
Poole & Sandbanks (pb)	1-85937-251-1	£9.99	Winchester (pb)	1-85937-428-x	£9.99
Preston (pb)	1-85937-212-0	£9.99	Windmills & Watermills	1-85937-242-2	£17.99
Reading (pb)	1-85937-238-4	£9.99	Worcester (pb)	1-85937-165-5	£9.99
Romford (pb)	1-85937-319-4	£9.99	Worcestershire	1-85937-152-3	£14.99
Salisbury (pb)	1-85937-239-2	£9.99	York (pb)	1-85937-199-x	£9.99
Scarborough (pb)	1-85937-379-8	£9.99	Yorkshire (pb)	1-85937-186-8	£9.99
St Albans (pb)	1-85937-341-0	£9.99	Yorkshire Living Memories	1-85937-166-3	£14.99

See Frith books on the internet www.francisfrith.co.uk

FRITH PRODUCTS & SERVICES

Francis Frith would doubtless be pleased to know that the pioneering publishing venture he started in 1860 still continues today. A hundred and forty years later, The Francis Frith Collection continues in the same innovative tradition and is now one of the foremost publishers of vintage photographs in the world. Some of the current activities include:

Interior Decoration

Today Frith's photographs can be seen framed and as giant wall murals in thousands of pubs, restaurants, hotels, banks, retail stores and other public buildings throughout the country. In every case they enhance the unique local atmosphere of the places they depict and provide reminders of gentler days in an increasingly busy and frenetic world.

Product Promotions

Frith products are used by many major companies to promote the sales of their own products or to reinforce their own history and heritage. Frith promotions have been used by Hovis bread, Courage beers, Scots Porage Oats, Colman's mustard, Cadbury's foods, Mellow Birds coffee, Dunhill pipe tobacco, Guinness, and Bulmer's Cider.

Genealogy and Family History

As the interest in family history and roots grows world-wide, more and more people are turning to Frith's photographs of Great Britain for images of the towns, villages and streets where their ancestors lived; and, of course, photographs of the churches and chapels where their ancestors were christened, married and buried are an essential part of every genealogy tree and family album.

Frith Products

All Frith photographs are available Framed or just as Mounted Prints and Posters (size 23 x 16 inches). These may be ordered from the address below. From time to time other products - Address Books, Calendars, Table Mats, etc - are available.

The Internet

Already twenty thousand Frith photographs can be viewed and purchased on the internet through the Frith websites and a myriad of partner sites.

For more detailed information on Frith companies and products, look at these sites:

www.francisfrith.co.uk
www.francisfrith.com
(for North American visitors)

See the complete list of Frith Books at:

www.francisfrith.co.uk

This web site is regularly updated with the latest list of publications from the Frith Book Company. If you wish to buy books relating to another part of the country that your local bookshop does not stock, you may purchase on-line.

For further information, trade, or author enquiries please contact us at the address below:
The Francis Frith Collection, Frith's Barn, Teffont, Salisbury, Wiltshire, England SP3 5QP.
Tel: +44 (0)1722 716 376 Fax: +44 (0)1722 716 881 Email: sales@francisfrith.co.uk

See Frith books on the internet www.francisfrith.co.uk

To receive your FREE Mounted Print

Mounted Print
Overall size 14 x 11 inches

Cut out this Voucher and return it with your remittance for £1.95 to cover postage and handling, to UK addresses. For overseas addresses please include £4.00 post and handling. Choose any photograph included in this book. Your SEPIA print will be A4 in size, and mounted in a cream mount with burgundy rule line, overall size 14 x 11 inches.

Order additional Mounted Prints at HALF PRICE (only £7.49 each*)

If there are further pictures you would like to order, possibly as gifts for friends and family, purchase them at half price (no additional postage and handling required).

Have your Mounted Prints framed*

For an additional £14.95 per print you can have your chosen Mounted Print framed in an elegant polished wood and gilt moulding, overall size 16 x 13 inches (no additional postage and handling required).

---

* IMPORTANT!
These special prices are only available if ordered using the original voucher on this page (no copies permitted) and at the same time as your free Mounted Print, for delivery to the same address

---

Frith Collectors' Guild

From time to time we publish a magazine of news and stories about Frith photographs and further special offers of Frith products. If you would like 12 months FREE membership, please return this form.

Send completed forms to:
The Francis Frith Collection, Frith's Barn, Teffont, Salisbury, Wiltshire SP3 5QP

Voucher for FREE and Reduced Price Frith Prints

Picture no.	Page number	Qty	Mounted @ £7.49	Framed + £14.95	Total Cost
		1	**Free of charge***	£	£
			£7.49	£	£
			£7.49	£	£
			£7.49	£	£
			£7.49	£	£
			£7.49	£	£

Please allow 28 days for delivery	*** Post & handling**	**£1.95**
Book Title	**Total Order Cost**	**£**

Please do not photocopy this voucher. Only the original is valid, so please cut it out and return it to us.

I enclose a cheque / postal order for £ . . . .
made payable to 'The Francis Frith Collection'
OR please debit my Mastercard / Visa / Switch / Amex card
(credit cards please on all overseas orders)

Number . . . .

Issue No(Switch only) . . . . .Valid from (Amex/Switch) . . . .

Expires . . . . Signature . . . .

Name Mr/Mrs/Ms . . . .

Address . . . .

. . . .

. . . .

. . . . Postcode . . . .

Daytime Tel No . . . .   Valid to 31/12/02

The Francis Frith Collectors' Guild

Please enrol me as a member for 12 months free of charge.

Name Mr/Mrs/Ms . . . .

Address . . . .

. . . .

. . . .

. . . . Postcode . . . .

Would you like to find out more about Francis Frith?

We have recently recruited some entertaining speakers who are happy to visit local groups, clubs and societies to give an illustrated talk documenting Frith's travels and photographs. If you are a member of such a group and are interested in hosting a presentation, we would love to hear from you.

Our speakers bring with them a small selection of our local town and county books, together with sample prints. They are happy to take orders. A small proportion of the order value is donated to the group who have hosted the presentation. The talks are therefore an excellent way of fundraising for small groups and societies.

Can you help us with information about any of the Frith photographs in this book?

We are gradually compiling an historical record for each of the photographs in the Frith archive. It is always fascinating to find out the names of the people shown in the pictures, as well as insights into the shops, buildings and other features depicted.

If you recognize anyone in the photographs in this book, or if you have information not already included in the author's caption, do let us know. We would love to hear from you, and will try to publish it in future books or articles.

Our production team

Frith books are produced by a small dedicated team at offices in the converted Grade II listed 18th-century barn at Teffont near Salisbury, illustrated above. Most have worked with the Frith Collection for many years. All have in common one quality: they have a passion for the Frith Collection. The team is constantly expanding, but currently includes:

Jason Buck, John Buck, Douglas Burns, Heather Crisp, Isobel Hall, Rob Hames, Hazel Heaton, Peter Horne, James Kinnear, Tina Leary, Hannah Marsh, Eliza Sackett, Terence Sackett, Sandra Sanger, Shelley Tolcher, Susanna Walker, Clive Wathen and Jenny Wathen.